"*I Was Ill and You Cared for Me* is a poignant, prayerful, and eminently inspiring meditation on how select biblical passages can be a source of comfort and consolation not only for those who are physically and mentally impaired, but also for their family, friends, and caregivers. Craghan is refreshingly honest about the fear, pain, sorrow, and sense of abandonment that afflict persons who are sick and dying—as well as those who love them—but is also resoundingly hopeful because the God who comes to us in Jesus never abandons us, even in death. Beautifully written and pastorally insightful, *I Was Ill and You Cared for Me* testifies that suffering, diminishment, and death are an inescapable part of life but, thanks to the resurrection, do not triumph. This book is a holy gift for anyone wrestling with the mystery of suffering and searching for reasons to hope."

> —Paul J. Wadell
> Professor of Religious Studies
> St. Norbert College, De Pere, Wisconsin

"Reflections for those who suffer are many. John Craghan directs his thoughts toward those who serve the sufferer. His reflections may have originated in the heart, but he has grounded them in the power and inspiration of the biblical tradition. Relatively short and to the point, they are filled with the sensitivity and empathy that he exhorts. Whether or not one directly serves those who suffer, this book calls all to compassion for human weakness."

> —Dianne Bergant, CSA
> Professor of Old Testament Studies
> Catholic Theological Union

"John Craghan's biblical reflections fill a great lacuna because they engage the imaginations of caregivers who pursue a spirituality of service to those who are impaired in some way. Whether we try to imagine our characters from biblical stories or focus on the visual objects and aesthetics of their dwellings, Craghan hits a balanced note of beauty, *praxis*, and compassion with his choices of images and of ways we are privileged to serve. His images are clear, practical, and theologically-based, and so he offers us much more than a script or guide to what to do . . . rather he advises us to imagine 'how to be' with these our sisters and brothers."

—John Endres, SJ
Jesuit School of Theology at Berkeley

# I Was Ill
# and
# You Cared for Me

Biblical Reflections on Serving
the Physically and Mentally Impaired

*John F. Craghan*

**LITURGICAL PRESS**
Collegeville, Minnesota

www.litpress.org

| 1 | 2 | 3 | 4 | 5 | 6 | 7 | 8 | 9 |
| --- | --- | --- | --- | --- | --- | --- | --- | --- |

**Library of Congress Cataloging-in-Publication Data**

Craghan, John F.
   I was ill and you cared for me : biblical reflections on serving the physically and mentally impaired / John F. Craghan.
      pages cm
    ISBN 978-0-8146-3767-8 — ISBN 978-0-8146-3792-0 (ebook)
    1. Church work with people with disabilities—Meditations.
   2. Caring—Religious aspects—Christianity—Meditations.   I. Title.
   BV4460.C73   2014
   259'.4—dc23                         2013037435

*For*
Rosemary Helen
*in*
solidarity and affection

# Contents

# Preface

These reflections stem from a variety of venues. Over the years I have observed the dedication and generosity of family members who minister at home to their loved ones suffering from debilitating physical and mental handicaps. I have also learned of the selfless service of hospice teams as they assist the dying and their families in hospitals, nursing facilities, and private homes. Over the last nine months I have visited a close friend, generally once a week, who because of his serious mental illness is now confined to a nursing home. These and similar experiences have led me to ponder the following teaching of Jesus: "I was . . . ill and you cared for me" (Matt 25:35-36). (This is part of Jesus' judgment of the nations [Matt 25:31-46] in which salvation or damnation depends on recognizing or not recognizing Jesus in the hungry, thirsty, etc.) I seek, therefore, to investigate the biblical resources that may speak to the challenge of caring for those physically and mentally impaired.

I frankly admit that I have very little expertise in clinical psychology or psychiatry. By training I am a biblicist, a person who has spent a lifetime studying the Sacred Scriptures. In this little work I offer the reader a variety of biblical reflections that may help family members, friends, and health care workers deal with the diminished physical and mental conditions of those they love and serve. I am fully aware of my limitations in this endeavor. To be sure, there are countless other biblical texts and themes that I could have explored. Nonetheless, I offer these to the reader with the fond hope that they may enrich in some small way their ministry of caring.

I dedicate these reflections to my sister-in-law who by her twice-daily nursing home visits to her husband of over fifty years teaches all of us courage and endurance in both the best of times and the worst of times. I also thank my wife Barbara Lynne for her patient and professional perusal of the manuscript and her many helpful suggestions.

John F. Craghan
Pentecost 2013

# Abbreviations
# for Biblical References

| | |
|---|---|
| 1 Cor | 1 Corinthians |
| 1 Kgs | 1 Kings |
| 2 Sam | 2 Samuel |
| Exod | Exodus |
| Gen | Genesis |
| Isa | Isaiah |
| Jer | Jeremiah |
| Lam | Lamentations |
| Matt | Matthew |
| Ps(s) | Psalm(s) |
| Rev | Revelation |
| Zeph | Zephaniah |

# Beyond Pity

## Entrances

There is a significant contrast between entering the venues of the physically and mentally impaired and other settings. For example, when attending a concert or musical, we notice the excitement of the people, their manner of dress, the warming-up session of the orchestra, and the dimming of the lights. When going to a major league baseball game, we observe the lush green of the infield and outfield, the players taking batting practice or shagging flies, the caps and shirts of the fans that define their team preference, the singing of the national anthem, and finally the announcement to play ball. If attending the pope's Angelus prayer and talk at St. Peter's in Rome, we experience the anxiety of the crowd, the jockeying for position to get a better view, the opening of the windows of the apostolic palace, the lowering of the papal tapestry, and finally the breathtaking appearance of the white-clad pontiff.

All of the above entrances clash with the entrance into the venues of the physically and mentally impaired. In visiting those at home, especially on the first occasion, we sense an eerie quiet. There is no longer the clamor and din of children and grandchildren. If there is music, it is very subdued. When the caregiver warmly greets us, the bravado and zest

1

of days gone by have vanished. If the venue is a nursing home, we watch the painfully slow movement of many residents in their wheel chairs. We also glimpse the lack of any real emotion in their faces. We may hear moans and groans emanating from their rooms. We conclude that the overall atmosphere is somber. Perhaps it is no exaggeration to say that we are in a kind of twilight zone.

In such settings the haunting cadences of the prophet Jeremiah's picture of the dismantling of creation (the threat of military invasion) comes easily to mind:

> I looked at the earth—it was waste and void;
>     at the heavens—their light had gone out!
> I looked at the mountains—they were quaking!
>     All the hills were crumbling!
> I looked—there was no one;
>     even the birds of the air had flown away!
> I looked—the garden land was a wilderness,
>     with all its cities destroyed
>     before the LORD, before his blazing anger.
> For thus says the LORD:
> The whole earth shall be waste,
>     but I will not wholly destroy it.
> Because of this the earth shall mourn,
>     the heavens above shall darken;
> I have spoken, I will not change my mind,
>     I have decided, I will not turn back. (Jer 4:23-28)

For Jeremiah the world has returned to chaos because of his people's disobedience. Each time the prophet looks at that world, he sees more and more of it returning to its condition prior to creation. The picture is bleak indeed: the disappearance of light, birds, fertility, and humanity. Our visit to the physically and mentally impaired may unfortunately resonate all too well with Jeremiah's gloomy description. Now the crumbling and quaking do not take place in the mountains or hills. Rather, they are now evident in the person or persons we are visiting. We sense waste and devastation, a reaction that may move us to mourn.

### The emergence of the loved one

When visiting a friend or loved one at home, we may receive a welcoming smile but the smile may demand a great effort to delve into his or her memory bank to recognize us. When we see this person either propped up in bed or seated in a comfortable chair supported by pillows, we may begin to think that this is not the person we once knew. The zest for life and laughter has greatly diminished. Our visit is Jeremiah revisited.

If visiting in a nursing home, we may catch a glimpse of our loved one at the end of a long corridor or lying in bed. What a stark contrast with his or her former self. Here, too, the energy and vitality have all disappeared. There is no longer any sense of personal engagement. The clash between before and after is overwhelming. We recall the sharp intellect of days gone by. We remember the dexterity of those fingers and hands in performing a multitude of different hobbies and jobs. We rehearse the accomplishments of the past from manual labor to musical talent. We miss the incessant energy. Without realizing it we are participating in Jeremiah's dismantling of creation.

Whether at home, a hospital, or a nursing facility, we can at times converse but at a radically reduced rate. The effort to articulate his or her thoughts is no doubt considerable. His or her mind is not infrequently focusing on the past so that the words and phrases in no way overlap with the intended conversation. We pause—perhaps reluctantly—and ponder this devastating loss. At this point we can appreciate the profound emotion expressed in David's elegy or funeral song on the occasion of the deaths of Saul and Jonathan at the hands of the treacherous Philistines:

> Alas! the glory of Israel,
>     slain upon your heights!
> How can the warriors have fallen! . . .
> Saul and Jonathan, beloved and dear,
>     separated neither in life nor death,
>     swifter than eagles, stronger than lions!
> Women of Israel, weep over Saul,
>     who clothed you in scarlet and in finery,
>     covered your clothing with ornaments of gold.
> How can the warriors have fallen
>     in the thick of battle!
>     Jonathan—slain upon your heights!
> I grieve for you, Jonathan my brother!
>     Most dear have you been to me; . . .
> How can the warriors have fallen,
>     the weapons of war have perished!
>                     (2 Sam 1:19, 23-25, 26a, 27)

The refrain ("How can the warriors have fallen!") appears all too appropriate. The whole scenario, whether at home, the hospital, or nursing facility makes absolutely no sense. These once vibrant and energetic people are woefully so much less than their former selves. Like Saul and Jonathan, our warrior friends and loved ones have experienced a form of death whereby everything seems surreal to us.

Because all too frequently our lives revolve around control and power, it may be too difficult to express grief. Frankly, we are losing our once intoxicating sense of control and power. We now confront a situation for which we are not adequately prepared. To make matters worse, we feel that outsiders will simply not understand. They are like the Phi-

listines in David's elegy who cannot begin to imagine what
it means to lose a Saul and a Jonathan.

In this flood of conflicting emotions we are too easily
tempted to believe that we are totally alone. We cannot begin
to fathom that Another stands by in a quiet and unobtrusive
way. Yet the biblical message of divine involvement is more
than a soothing gesture or quick fix.

To his distraught people the prophet Zephaniah envisions
the transforming power of confidence in Jerusalem's future:

> Do not fear, Zion,
>     do not be discouraged!
> The LORD, your God, is in your midst,
>     a mighty savior
> Who will rejoice over you with gladness,
>     and renew you in his love. (Zeph 3:16b-17)

To his exilic audience languishing in Babylon Second Isaiah
proclaims: "Fear not, for I am with you" (Isa 43:5a). According to Matthew, Jesus bears the title "Emmanuel" that
means "God is with us" (Matt 1:23). In the very last line of
the same gospel, the departing Jesus solemnly announces:
"And behold, I am with you always" (Matt 28:20). "With"
is the preposition of reassuring love. In the midst of our despair and frustration we are challenged to acknowledge One
who is ever present despite the deafening sound of silence.

At this stage of our ordeal we are urged to move beyond
pity for our loved ones and self-pity for ourselves ("There
but for the grace of God go I"). The situation now calls for a
demanding strategy that is nothing less than a call to prayer
but a form of prayer that is totally honest and hope-oriented.
It is time for the prayer of lament.

# How Long, O Lord? How Long?

## Coopting the biblical lament

At prayer we confront the issues of daily life. In the presence of our God we must dismiss all fakery and make-believe. We acknowledge that our frustration is genuine and that a steely effort to block it out will only add to the situation. In opening ourselves up to our God, we dare to face life with all its agony. We cannot resort to a never-never land where pain does not exist and anguish is not genuine. In the face of physical and mental impairment we have to admit that the bottom is falling out of life. Ironically the agony and frustration of such illness can now become the new raw material for prayer.

Approximately one third of the book of Psalms falls into the category of lament, whether individual or communal. (Laments also occur elsewhere: in Jeremiah and Lamentations, for example.) This very number more than suggests that Israel could not escape the reality of pain and sorrow. What is noteworthy, however, is that these laments do not merely catalog or enumerate the many forms of human anguish from the more sustainable to the more unbearable. (They are not what today we would call a "gripe session.") Far from being a database of life's slings and arrows, the laments represent a tragically human form of appeal. They are addressed to Someone who formerly showed interest in his people's plight but now seems to have abdicated the scene. Nonetheless these prayers articulate a hope, at times vibrant but at other times less so, that God will intervene and redress the situation. In other words, the laments pursue a movement that follows up the vivid images of excruciating pain with petition and finally praise.

Hurt that cannot be expressed is hurt that cannot be healed. In lashing out against its God, Israel dares to hope that this partner will take these more than upsetting scenes seriously and intervene. The very act of venting its sufferings is the implicit realization that the Lord can do something and hopefully will do something to comfort and console. Confronted with physical and mental impairment, we must accept the challenge to lament.

In the biblical lament the Lord thus becomes the God of our problem. What the laments actually presuppose is that our problem becomes God's problem. Far from being uninvolved, the Lord continues to take a genuine interest in us and thereby remains a committed partner. The very fact that there is a God who addresses our problem means the death of loneliness and isolation. We are linked to Another. Whether at home, in the hospital, or in the nursing home there is no divine isolation ward, although it may seem so at times.

The laments in the book of Psalms reveal the following basic structure: address with an introductory cry for help; the lament itself, namely, the problem or problems of the petitioner; confession of trust or assurance of being heard; petition; vow of praise. While it is difficult to explain the transition from distress to relief, what is usually clear is the transformation of the petitioner.

A caveat: in praying the psalms and especially the laments, we must always realize that they are poetry. The poet does not make intellectual statements. Instead, he employs symbols and images, allowing and even challenging those at prayer to picture multiple images and endless possibilities. The poet's choice of words thus enables the petitioners to experience such emotions as fear, pain, and desperation. The imagination plays an extremely vital role in these prayers.

> How long, LORD? Will you utterly forget me?
>     How long will you hide your face from me?
> How long must I carry sorrow in my soul,
>     grief in my heart day after day?
>     How long will my enemy triumph over me?
>
> Look upon me, answer me, LORD, my God!
>     Give light to my eyes lest I sleep in death,
> Lest my enemy say, "I have prevailed,"
>     lest my foes rejoice at my downfall.
>
> But I trust in your mercy.
>     Grant my heart joy in your salvation,
> I will sing to the LORD,
>     for he has dealt bountifully with me! (Ps 13)

Psalm 13 admirably introduces the focus of this chapter. In verses 2-3, the lingering question "how long" appears no less than four times. From the very start, therefore, something has gone horribly wrong in the life of the speaker as well as in the life of the speaker with God. Evidently he has no qualms about blaming the Lord for this debacle whatever the precise problem is. This Lord is guilty of crass forgetfulness and negligent absence (v. 2). This sad state of affairs has led to the speaker's sorrow, grief, and the triumph of the enemy (v. 3).

There are no niceties of speech in this psalm, only a barrage of attacks on the One responsible. In verse 4 the speaker petitions the Lord to consider, respond, and enlighten. The conjunction "lest" in verses 4b-5 succeeds in making the psalmist's problem the Lord's problem. These statements supply the data on the basis of which the Lord must inexorably act. Then a pause follows: a period of waiting, perhaps a long period followed by divine intervention. Such intervention works hand in hand with trust, a joyful heart, and a song (v. 6). The final words capture the speaker's new frame of mind: "for he has dealt bountifully with me."

All those suffering from the physical and mental impairment of their loved ones can easily transfer the pathos of this psalm to their own situation. They continually ask how long their loved one must undergo this torment and how long they themselves must deal with this tragedy. These new speakers in the psalm must rightly petition their God to consider, respond, and enlighten. They can also legitimately dare to trust and eventually sing. Unfortunately the pause and the waiting will not immediately disappear. To express rage and upset is nonetheless to acknowledge the presence of this God. They must never cease to cry out and make their case heard.

> How many are my foes, LORD!
>    How many rise against me!
> How many say of me,
>    "There is no salvation for him in God."
>
> But you, LORD, are a shield around me;
>    my glory, you keep my head high.
>
> With my own voice I will call out to the LORD,
>    and he will answer me from his holy mountain.
>
> I lie down and I fall asleep,
>    [and] I will wake up, for the LORD sustains me.
> I do not fear, then, thousands of people
>    arrayed against me on every side.

Arise, Lord! Save me, my God!
   For you strike the cheekbone of all my foes;
   you break the teeth of the wicked.
Salvation is from the Lord!
   May your blessing be upon your people! (Ps 3)

This psalm involves three characters: the Lord, the psalm-ist, and "the enemies" or a great variety of possible foes and associated problems. Attacked by these implacable op-ponents who deny all possibility of divine intervention, the psalmist appeals to the Lord (vv. 2-4). He identifies this God as a powerful military figure (v. 4, "my shield") who will heed his call and respond (v. 5). The psalmist's sleep (v. 6) symbolizes the profound hope and expectation of God's timely aid. Though his enemies rise against him (v. 2), he pleads: "Arise, Lord! Save me, my God! (v. 8). Employing martial imagery, the psalmist depicts the Lord as striking the cheekbone and breaking the teeth of his opponents. It is only a matter of time before the Lord fulfills the author's hope.

The loved ones of the physically and mentally impaired will easily resonate with the "how many" in verses 2-3. The enemies now take on the concrete form of the insidious components of serious physical and mental illness that affect their loved ones. Perhaps the military metaphor of the Lord as a shield may not appeal. Instead, the image of the Lord as a comforting friend or confidant may be an improvement. Despite seemingly insurmountable obstacles the symbol of sleep suggests the very basis of hope. The Lord's military initiative in verse 8 may imply final and definitive involve-ment that creates an atmosphere of acceptance in contrast to the enemies' attacks at the beginning of the psalm. In the final analysis the psalm is a powerful appeal for God to get involved. The home caregivers as well as those in hospitals and nursing homes must be relentless in bringing these petitions to the attention of their God.

> How solitary sits the city,
>     once filled with people.
> She who was great among the nations
>     is now like a widow.
> Once a princess among the provinces,
>     now a toiling slave.
> She weeps incessantly in the night,
>     her cheeks damp with tears.
> She has no one to comfort her
>     from all her lovers;
> Her friends have all betrayed her,
>     and become her enemies.
>
> Judah has gone into exile,
>     after oppression and harsh labor;
> She dwells among the nations,
>     yet finds no rest:
> All her pursuers overtake her
>     in the narrow straits.
>
> The roads to Zion mourn,
>     empty of pilgrims to her feasts.
> All her gateways are desolate,
>     her priests groan,
> Her young women grieve;
>     her lot is bitter.
>
> Her foes have come out on top,
>     her enemies are secure;
> Because the LORD has afflicted her
>     for her many rebellions.
> Her children have gone away,
>     captive before the foe. (Lam 1:1-5)

The Book of Lamentations responds to the devastation of the city of Jerusalem in 586 BC at the hands of the invading Babylonian army. The five poems in this book capture the pathos and depression of God's people. With the destruction of the temple in particular, they endure physical and mental impairment. In this opening passage an unidentified narrator reports what he actually sees. He persuades the reader to accept his view on the city's suffering. For him it is all so sad because Jerusalem has brought all this on herself.

The very first word "how" is key: how could this possibly have happened to Jerusalem/Zion? It is a tragedy of such magnitude that speech becomes muffled. In the rest of the verse, the narrator shocks the reader by contrasting the past with the present. The city once filled with people, like a pregnant woman, is now like a widow. Like a widow, she lacks a husband and possibly a family to support her. Having once been a princess, she is now the slave of a foreign power. Her weeping never stops but, worst of all, there is no one to comfort her (v. 2). As Jerusalem/Zion weeps, the nation goes into exile where they are oppressed, cast out among the nations, and overtaken by pursuers (v. 3).

The grief experienced by the city has become such a powerful force that even the roads and gateways succumb to her grief. Since the people can no longer worship at the temple, the city has, in effect, lost her soul. Priests and young women also groan and break down in tears. It is almost an understatement to say "her lot is bitter" (v. 4). Her sorrow deepens as her foes wrench her children away and lead them into captivity. The narrator is compelled to note that the Lord has brought these calamities upon her because of her rebellions (v. 5).

For the loved ones of the physically and mentally impaired the sentiments of this lamentation match their own, perhaps unexpressed feelings to some extent. They too raise the question: how could all this have happened? The contrast between the pregnant woman and the widow symbolizes their grief almost to the point where the present shadowy figure of their loved ones seems unrecognizable. The emphasis on groaning and weeping in this passage corresponds to their own state of frustration and abandonment. They too experience the plight of Jerusalem/Zion because there may be no one to comfort and console. Just as the people cannot worship because of the destruction of the temple, they too find it exceedingly difficult to worship because their God seems to have abandoned them at such a crucial time. While Jerusalem/Zion deserves her fate because of her sinfulness, the loved ones and friends continue to protest their innocence and wonder why they too are the gutted city bereft of support and consolation.

Unlike Psalms 3 and 13, this first poem in Lamentations does not conclude on a note of hope. It is more an objective report or recital of everything that went wrong. At this point there is no light at the end of the tunnel. However, in the third poem the poet writes:

> The LORD's acts of mercy are not exhausted,
>     his compassion is not spent;
> They are renewed each morning—
>     great is your faithfulness. (Lam 3:22-23)

For the first time in this biblical book the author addresses God directly, giving the impression that he has been there all along. But now the poet bursts into creedal statements. The Lord's love and concern is not over. In fact, it is renewed every morning. Faithfulness is the Lord's badge of honor. In the midst of the ashes and smoldering wreckage, there is yet hope.

For the loved ones and friends of the physically and mentally impaired these verses must strike a note of hope, but a hope without immediate fulfillment. The divine assurance is there, but the divine decisive action is still wanting. As in Psalm 13, they plead: "How long, LORD?" This elusive God is compassion personified, but not one who operates according to our human timetables. This state of affairs must continue to prompt these questions: is anybody there? Does anybody care?

### Contrasting the grief and death process and the laments

The work of Elizabeth Kübler-Ross on the grief and death process is well-known. The overview of the biblical laments in this chapter may help the caregivers, loved ones, and friends of the physically and mentally impaired compare their approach with that of Kübler-Ross. Hopefully the contrasts will reveal the positive components in the Bible's approach to pain and suffering.

In place of denial the laments insist on address. Thus the laments are directed to Someone who is interested, whereas the grief process focuses on the unreality of the pain and the anguish. Whereas depression sets in as an element of the grief process, expression takes over in the laments. Israel expects that her plea will get a hearing and her expression bears this out. Unlike the grief process, the laments are grounded in a framework of relationship. It is not a question of being alone in a nursing facility or hospital bed or of being abandoned at home by the family. In the laments, an "I" and "Thou" always pervades: relationships are central. As a result, the laments always look forward to intervention. The laments imply that we are treated as persons even in our most vulnerable situations. The grief process lacks that frame of reference.

**Writing your own laments**

It may be extremely helpful to attempt to write your own laments. It can prove to be a cathartic exercise. It will be useful to begin by reading some of the biblical laments. Next, proceed to express your frustrations and anger as well as your hope for deliverance after the manner of the biblical models. After completing your lament, you may choose to put it aside for a while. Reread it later, perhaps when your anxiety has passed and you feel more in control. An excellent guide for writing your own laments is *Psalms of Lament,* by Ann Weems (Louisville, KY: Westminster John Knox, 1995).

# The Sacrament of Touch

## Introduction

In our society touching is a "touchy" issue. In our Western world people do not touch each other as spontaneously or readily as people in other cultures. As a matter of fact, in our society we prefer not to get too close to other people.

In addition to touches for love and intimacy as well as sexual arousal, touching performs other roles. For example, there are functional or professional touches—physicians, barbers, beauticians are examples that easily come to mind. There are also social-polite touches, the most common of which in our society is the handshake. Such a gesture communicates a sense of friendship. Finally there are gestures that articulate warmth and closeness such as holding hands, embracing, kissing.

## Jesus as model of the sacrament of touch

Jesus exemplifies the warmth/closeness dimension of touch in Mark 10:13-16. In this episode the disciples rebuke the people who are bringing their children to Jesus to have him touch them. Becoming indignant, Jesus announces that the kingdom of God belongs to people like children. The

16

scene concludes: "Then he embraced them and blessed them, placing his hands on them" (v. 16). Jesus offers a negative instance of the social-polite touch when he rebukes his host, Simon the Pharisee, for not giving him a kiss when invited to dine with him (Luke 7:45).

Jesus exemplifies the functional or professional touch in his miracles. (Such touches are aptly termed therapeutic.) It is noteworthy that in his miracles Jesus associates particularly with the physically and mentally impaired: the blind, the lame, the lepers, the deaf, the dead, and the demoniacs (see Matt 11:5; Luke 7:22). Most of the time Jesus effects healing by a simple word (see Mark 5:42), but touching also plays a prominent role.

Jesus cures the blind man of Bethsaida in stages. First, Jesus takes him by the hand, leads him outside the village, and puts spittle on his eyes. Second, "he laid his hands on his eyes a second time and he saw clearly" (Mark 8:25a). In Mark, Jesus encounters a leper whose very sight stirs him to compassion. He then proceeds to stretch out his hand and touch him. "The leprosy left him immediately, and he was made clean" (Mark 1:42). He puts his fingers into the ears of a speech-impaired deaf man, applies spittle, and touches his tongue. "And [immediately] the man's eyes were opened, his speech impediment was removed, and he spoke plainly" (Mark 7:35). Jesus takes the dead daughter of Jairus by the hand and commands her to arise. "The girl, a child of twelve, arose immediately and walked around" (Mark 5:42a).

In all these instances power is assumed to reside in Jesus and contact with him can thus effect physical healing. By not hesitating to touch those who are suffering, Jesus reveals his utter humanity. To reach out and make contact with the sick is to fulfill his mission of proclaiming the Good News. As he expresses it in his inaugural sermon in the Nazareth synagogue,

he (the Spirit of the Lord) has anointed me
  to bring glad tidings to the poor.
He has sent me to proclaim liberty to captives
  and recovery of sight to the blind. (Luke 4:18)

Among other healing methods, touch plays a considerable role in this aspect of his ministry.

### Other ministers of the sacrament of touch

Admittedly we humans cannot perform Jesus' therapeutic miracles. Nonetheless, we can serve as his ministers of the sacrament of touch. Obviously, sacrament in this sense is not to be identified with the seven sacraments. Yet like them, sacrament as used here is both a sign and an instrument. It is a sign of God's presence: in this instance, of his presence to the physically and mentally impaired. It is an awareness of the innate goodness of these people. It is also an instrument insofar as it communicates the special bond linking the physically and mentally impaired to their caregivers, loved ones, and friends.

This understanding of the sacramentality of touch responds to this question: How do we reconnect with Jesus who has gone home to the Father? To be sure, the seven sacraments link us to Jesus, especially in the Eucharist. However, the sacrament of touch also functions as a form of mediation between the heavenly Jesus and his earthly extended family. When caregivers, loved ones, and friends exercise their ministry of touch, they reveal the intimate family bond that links Jesus to his suffering family members.

Whenever caregivers, loved ones, and friends hold the hand of a physically or mentally impaired person, they are making Jesus present to him or her. Whenever they raise a sunken face, they proclaim the message of Jesus who opposes everything that oppresses and depresses the human spirit. Whenever they shake hands, they announce that Jesus' kingdom is still being realized. Whenever they fluff a pillow, they repeat the words of Jesus: "Come to me, all you who labor and are burdened, and I will give you rest" (Matt 11:28). Whenever they hug a physically or mentally impaired person, they make real Jesus' promise to be with us always (Matt 28:20). There is no special ordination or institutional ritual for this form of ministry. It derives from the compassionate mission of Jesus who solemnly proclaims: "whatever you did for one of these least brothers of mine, you did for me" (Matt 25:40). To tease a smile on the face of the physically and mentally impaired is nothing less than the accomplishment of a lifetime. To put it another way, God could not be everywhere, so God created ministers of the sacrament of touch.

# Deck the Halls!

### The role of symbols

Symbols abound in our world. The president, governor, and others like to attach a plaque to their podium to remind their audiences of their office. Flags, whether those of office, sport clubs, or teams remind us—very powerfully at times—of our sense of loyalty and values. Emma Lazarus's poem ("Give me your tired and your poor, your huddled masses yearning to breathe free") captures the symbolism of the Statue of Liberty in New York harbor. Symbols thus tell us who we are and how we should act.

Many Christian homes usually have a generous supply of family photos, pieces of art, and various kinds of mementoes. Naturally caregivers assume that this tranquil atmosphere will bring back old memories to the physically and mentally impaired in their charge. They are pleasant reminders of the good old days. Unfortunately, not a few Christian homes lack some kind of religious symbol. Crosses/crucifixes, pictures of Jesus and Mary, statues of the saints, or other similar symbols are conspicuous by their absence. While family photos and the like play a necessary role, religious artifacts also merit a privileged place. They challenge all in the household to recall God's involvement and concern. In this sense, a religious picture is worth more than a thousand words.

Many nonsectarian hospitals and nursing homes employ a variety of paintings and pictures to create an upbeat climate. Clearly their intention is to add a dimension of joy and contentment for the physically and mentally impaired in their care. Sometimes, however, these choice works by famous artists and photographers stand in stark contrast to the physical and mental condition of the residents. Norman Rockwell, for example, has certainly captured the sense of America and his works amuse us and make us smile. However, are there any other images that can complement such works and also speak to the needs of the physically and mentally impaired? In other words, can we decorate with other pieces of art that reflect both the pain and the hope of the physically and mentally impaired and their loved ones? From an enormous possible pool, I select three biblical scenes and one non-biblical scene that, in my judgment, depict the frustration and the longing of all those involved.

### The cross

Most of the hospitals and nursing homes I am acquainted with are nonsectarian and consequently do not sponsor religious art. As noted above, many Christian homes lack religious symbols. However, since this is my wish list to address these lacunae, I begin with the cross. All too often the cross has become a meaningless piece of ecclesiastical furniture or a bland form of jewelry. We have to recall that crucifixion was a Roman form of capital punishment that made the victim suffer the maximum indignity. Employed as a deterrent because of its cruelty, it was nearly always inflicted on the lower classes, including slaves, violent criminals, and unruly elements in the provinces. For Romans, Greeks, Jews, and barbarians, the cross symbolized an extremely offensive attack on a human being. Hence a crucified Messiah was viewed as a contradiction in terms. But that is precisely what we find in the passion narrative:

> So Pilate, wishing to satisfy the crowd, released Barabbas to them and, after he had Jesus scourged, handed him over to be crucified.
>
> The soldiers led him away inside the palace, that is, the praetorium, and assembled the whole cohort. They clothed him in purple and, weaving a crown of thorns, placed it on him. They began to salute him with, "Hail, King of the Jews!" and kept striking his head with a reed and spitting upon him. They knelt before him in homage. And when they had mocked him, they stripped him of the purple cloak, dressed him in his own clothes, and led him out to crucify him.
>
> They pressed into service a passer-by, Simon, a Cyrenian, who was coming in from the country, the father of Alexander and Rufus, to carry his cross.
>
> They brought him to the place of Golgotha (which is translated Place of the Skull). They gave him wine drugged with myrrh, but he did not take it. Then they crucified him and divided his garments by casting lots for them to see what each should take. It was nine o'clock in the morning when they crucified him. The inscription of the charge against him read, "The King of the Jews." With him they crucified two revolutionaries, one on his right and one on his left. Those passing by reviled him, shaking their heads and saying, "Aha! You who would destroy the temple and rebuild it in three days, save yourself by coming down from the cross." Likewise the chief priests, with the scribes, mocked him among themselves and said, "He saved others; he cannot save himself. Let the Messiah, the King of Israel, come down now from the cross that we may see and believe." Those who were crucified with him also kept abusing him.
>
> At noon darkness came over the whole land until three in the afternoon. And at three o'clock Jesus cried out in a loud

voice, "*Eloi, Eloi, lema sabachthani?*" which is translated, "My God, my God, why have you forsaken me?" Some of the bystanders who heard it said, "Look, he is calling Elijah." One of them ran, soaked a sponge with wine, put it on a reed, and gave it to him to drink, saying, "Wait, let us see if Elijah comes to take him down." Jesus gave a loud cry and breathed his last. The veil of the sanctuary was torn in two from top to bottom. When the centurion who stood facing him saw how he breathed his last he said, "Truly this man was the Son of God!" (Mark 15:15-39)

In verses 15-21 Jesus is first flogged and then undergoes the mockery of the soldiers who dress him in a purple cloak and place a crown of thorns on his head. The soldiers judge the cloak and the crown appropriate since Jesus is charged with being the King of the Jews. After saluting him as such, the soldiers strike his head with a reed, spit on him, and kneel before him in mock homage. He is next forced to carry the crossbeam or lateral beam to the place of execution. However, his physical condition has so deteriorated that the soldiers force a passerby by the name of Simon of Cyrene to carry it for Jesus.

The loved ones and friends of the physically and mentally impaired can easily apply these verses to their own situation. Mockery takes on many vicious shapes and forms. Outsiders may simply observe that the time has come to let him/her go. In their view the person no longer contributes to society and is, therefore, dispensable. They will not volunteer their services after the manner of Simon of Cyrene in order to lighten the burden.

At Golgotha Jesus is further humiliated when he is crucified with two revolutionaries on either side after the manner of royal attendants. The mockery and taunts continue: first passersby, then the chief priests and scribes, and finally the two revolutionaries. At 3 p.m. Jesus cries out the beginning of Psalm 22: "My God, my God, why have you abandoned me?" These words serve a twofold purpose: they reveal Jesus' real suffering and they articulate his trust in God's power to save the innocent sufferer (the theme of the second half of Psalm 22). Jesus makes both elements of the psalm his own. Though enduring immense suffering, he retains the utmost confidence in his Father. Finally Jesus lets out a loud cry and breathes his last. The loud cry expresses the state of one in great physical pain. The suffering of Jesus has reached its climax, but the surprise of Easter morning still awaits Mark's audience.

The physically and mentally impaired as well as their loved ones and friends join Jesus in this cry of dereliction: "My God, my God, why have you abandoned me?" This is the darkest of hours when their God appears to be hiding and not on the scene. However, they must pursue the second half of the psalm, namely, trust in God's power to save the innocent sufferer. They must do more than look for a silver lining. They must dare to envision the empty tomb that will swallow up their grief and generate new life.

### The travelers on the road to Emmaus

Now that very day two of them were going to a village seven miles from Jerusalem called Emmaus, and they were conversing about all the things that had occurred. And it happened that while they were conversing and debating, Jesus himself drew near and walked with them, but their eyes were prevented from recognizing him. He asked them, "What are you discussing as you walk along?" They stopped, looking downcast. One of them, named Cleopas, said to him in reply, "Are you the only visitor to Jerusalem who does not know of the things that have taken place there in these days?" And he replied to them, "What sort of things?" They said to him, "The things that happened to Jesus the Nazarene, who was a prophet mighty in deed and word before God and all the people, how our chief priests and rulers both handed him over to a sentence of death and crucified him. But we were hoping that he would be the one to redeem Israel; and besides all this, it is now the third day since this took place. Some women from our group, however, have astounded us: they were at the tomb early in the morning and did not find his body; they came back and reported that they had indeed seen a vision of angels who announced that he was alive. Then some of those with us went to the tomb and found things just as the women had described, but him they did not see." And he said to them, "Oh, how foolish you are! How slow of heart to believe all that the prophets spoke! Was it not necessary that the Messiah should suffer these things and enter into his glory?" Then beginning with Moses and all the prophets, he interpreted to them what referred to him in all the scriptures. As they approached the village to which they were going, he gave the impression that he was going on farther. But they urged him, "Stay with us, for it is nearly evening and the day is almost over." So he went in to stay with them. And it happened that, while he was with them at table, he took bread, said the blessing, broke it, and gave it to them. With that their eyes were opened and they recognized him, but he vanished from their sight. Then they said to each other, "Were not our hearts burning [within us] while he spoke to us on the way and opened the scriptures to us?" So they set out at once and returned to Jerusalem where they found gathered together the eleven and those with them who were saying, "The Lord has truly been raised and has appeared to Simon!" Then the two recounted what had taken place on the way and how he was made known to them in the breaking of the bread. (Luke 24:13-35)

The two travelers on the road to Emmaus reflect initial sadness because of the events of Good Friday. These events have wiped out their hopes for Jesus' role as Israel's redeemer. They then inform the unrecognized Jesus of the women's report about the empty tomb. At this point Jesus begins to explain the nexus between death and resurrection. He clearly states that, in order to enter into his glory, the Messiah had first to suffer. After Jesus' disappearance, the two travelers return to Jerusalem to inform the eleven and those with them of their astounding encounter with Jesus. The recipients find this old news and proceed to tell the Emmaus travelers of Jesus' appearance to Peter.

Suffering and glory almost seem to be contradictory. The problem faced by the Emmaus travelers is also the one that challenges the loved ones and friends of the physically and mentally impaired. Faced with the painful reality of deteriorating health, they are challenged to cast their gaze away from the cross to the empty tomb. The Jesus transformed by the Resurrection becomes their anchor or safety net as they puzzle over the intrinsic link between the frustration of today's pain and the promise of a new life. It is much more than the thrill of victory and the agony of defeat. It is now a question of ultimately identifying the physically and mentally impaired with the Jesus revealed to the Emmaus travelers. The celebration of Eucharist must ground the anticipation of the eventual transformation of the physically and mentally impaired. As Luke puts it after the Eucharistic meal Jesus shared with his disciples on the way to Emmaus, "With that their eyes were opened and they recognized him, but he vanished from their sight" (Luke 24:31).

### The new heaven and the new earth

Then I saw a new heaven and a new earth. The former heaven and the former earth had passed away, and the sea was no more. I also saw the holy city, a new Jerusalem, coming down out of heaven from God, prepared as a bride adorned for her husband. I heard a loud voice from the throne saying, "Behold, God's dwelling is with the human race. He will dwell with them and they will be his people and God himself will always be with them [as their God]. He will wipe every tear from their eyes, and there shall be no more death or mourning, wailing or pain, [for] the old order has passed away." (Rev 21:1-4)

Composed by an unknown Christian prophet toward the end of the first century AD, Revelation addresses seven Christian communities in the Roman province of Asia (modern western Turkey). While the book speaks of martyrs and, therefore, of Roman persecution, the prevailing danger is nothing less than Roman imperial ideology (Caesar, not God, is divine). Resistance, not compromise with the Roman mores, is the only way, indeed a form of resistance that includes martyrdom and witness, but not violence. Despite the bleakness of the situation, the author insists that the righteous faithful will ultimately prevail.

In this passage the author of Revelation expresses hope by presenting a vision of the new world and the new Jerusalem, a vision calculated to encourage the persecuted Christian communities. The sea, often the symbol of opposition to God, is now vanquished. The holy city of Jerusalem, God's special handiwork, descends from its place of origin, namely, heaven. A voice explains the significance of the vision, that is, God's dwelling among his people. Indeed God will always be with them. With the passing away of the former world, the distress associated with it must also pass away. Hence God will eliminate fear, mourning, wailing, pain, and death. Finally in verse 5 God speaks for the very first time. He corroborates the explanation already given: "Behold, I make all things new."

The vision of the new heaven and the new earth is not a form of amnesia to help family members and friends forget the trauma of the present moment. Rather, it is the challenge to envision a God who sympathizes with human agony and offers graces to cope with the raw pain of physical and mental impairment. In a sense it is a manifesto that urges them not merely to accept the situation stoically but to engage themselves in God's capacity to provide. The new heaven and the new earth symbolize God's transforming power in the restoration of the future lives of the physically and mentally impaired.

### The icon of Our Mother of Perpetual Help

This Byzantine icon depicts Mary tenderly but tenaciously clutching her young son Jesus. The boy has just had a vision of his forthcoming passion: the archangel Gabriel holding a cross with three horizontal crossbeams and four nails at its foot and the archangel Michael holding the lance, the pole with a sponge, and a vessel of vinegar. Terribly frightened by this vision, the young boy has run to the safety of his mother's embrace. His right sandal is falling off his foot because he has run so fast. He holds his mother's right hand, seeking support and security. Mary's eyes gaze outward. However, she does not look at her Son but at her Son's extended family. Her eyes reflect compassion for all those, including her Son, who need help. She is Our Mother of Perpetual Help.

In this icon Mary represents the feminine dimension of God's compassion. As such, she is ever ready to help all of her Son's sisters and brothers, no matter what their problem. To the family and friends of the physically and mentally impaired she provides the same understanding and comfort she offered to her Son in this icon. She waits only to be asked and, when asked, is prompt to help, although the help may take time and reveal itself in different ways. Mothers enjoy that unique capacity to listen and then act. Our Mother of Perpetual Help belongs to this circle of mothers.

### Selecting your special symbol

The four symbols discussed above do not exhaust the multitude of religious images. They are merely an appeal to the loved ones and friends of the physically and mentally impaired to search for those symbols that address their concrete needs. In the end it should be a symbol that combines these two elements: the reality of pain and suffering and the hope for divine intervention.

# Chapter Five

# The Mystery of Divine Presence

### Introduction

We usually think of mystery as something utterly impenetrable, something that defies our human minds to solve. According to Pope Paul VI, a mystery is a reality imbued with the hidden presence of God. This leads us to pose the following question: where and how is God to be found? To put it another way, how can we get in touch with this God who always seems to be so elusive? After all, for most of us it is presence, not absence, that makes the heart grow fonder.

A first approach to these questions seems to be sacred space. In other words, there are certain locales where, at least according to tradition, God has appeared or is thought to have appeared. Consequently these places or locales have assumed an aura of holiness or sacredness. In American civil religion, for example, Plymouth Rock, Arlington Cemetery, the Statue of Liberty, the Capitol, to name only a few, are sacred American spaces because of their association with the American way of thinking and its subsequent values. Our history teaches us that we can identify our democratic principles in some way with these sacred American places.

### Sacred space in the Bible

Jacob departed from Beer-sheba and proceeded toward Haran. When he came upon a certain place, he stopped there for the night, since the sun had already set. Taking one of the stones at the place, he put it under his head and lay down in that place. Then he had a dream: a stairway rested on the ground, with its top reaching to the heavens; and God's angels were going up and down on it. And there was the LORD standing beside him and saying: I am the LORD, the God of Abraham your father and the God of Isaac; the land on which you are lying I will give to you and your descendants. Your descendants will be like the dust of the earth, and through them you will spread to the west and the east, to the north and the south. In you and your descendants all the families of the earth will find blessing. I am with you and will protect you wherever you go, and bring you back to this land. I will never leave you until I have done what I promised you. (Gen 28:10-15)

In this scene at Bethel, Jacob has experienced the presence of the God of the fathers. He acknowledges that God is truly in this place. This leads him to exclaim: "How awesome this place is! This is nothing else but the house of God [Bethel], the gateway to heaven!" (Gen 28:17).

Meanwhile Moses was tending the flock of his father-in-law Jethro, the priest of Midian. Leading the flock beyond the wilderness, he came to the mountain of God, Horeb. There the angel of the LORD appeared to him as fire flaming out of a bush. When he looked, although the bush was on fire, it was not being consumed. So Moses decided, "I must turn aside to look at this remarkable sight. Why does the bush not burn up?" When the LORD saw that he had turned aside to look, God called out to him from the bush: Moses! Moses! He answered, "Here I am." God said: Do not come near!

Remove your sandals from your feet, for the place where you stand is holy ground. (Exod 3:1-5)

In this tradition the place of the burning bush is called Horeb. Elsewhere it is named Sinai. The place is truly sacred space for two reasons. First, it is the place where God commissions Moses to deliver his people from Egyptian bondage. Second, it is the place where in Exodus 19 God enters into a covenant, a solemn relationship with the people of Israel. To experience Horeb/Sinai is to tread on hallowed ground. This is a place exceptionally marked with divine presence and hence divine holiness.

> "Is God indeed to dwell on earth? If the heavens and the highest heavens cannot contain you, how much less this house which I have built! Regard kindly the prayer and petition of your servant, LORD, my God, and listen to the cry of supplication which I, your servant, utter before you this day. May your eyes be open night and day toward this house, the place of which you said, My name shall be there; listen to the prayer your servant makes toward this place. Listen to the petition of your servant and of your people Israel which they offer toward this place. Listen, from the place of your enthronement, heaven, listen and forgive. (1 Kgs 8:27-30)

This passage is part of Solomon's prayer on the occasion of the dedication of the temple in Jerusalem. According to the author, the faithful pray in the temple but God hears their prayer from heaven, his dwelling place. To avoid too crude a notion of divine presence, this tradition states that God's name resides in the temple. Wherever the name of the Lord is uttered, God is present there because that name expresses and represents the person of God.

> Jesus answered and said to them, "Destroy this temple and in three days I will raise it up." The Jews said, "This temple

has been under construction for forty-six years, and you will raise it up in three days?" But he was speaking about the temple of his body. Therefore, when he was raised from the dead, his disciples remembered that he had said this, and they came to believe the scripture and the word Jesus had spoken. (John 2:19-22)

This passage is part of Jesus' cleansing of the temple in the gospel of John. By the time this gospel is written, the privilege of the Jerusalem temple (destroyed by the Romans in 70 AD), the seat of the divine presence, is transferred to the body of Jesus. Divine presence, therefore, has undergone significant development. This passage in John is not unlike Revelation 21:22 where there is no temple in the new Jerusalem "for its temple is the Lord God almighty and the Lamb."

### Divine presence in nearby churches

After visiting the physically and mentally impaired, whether at home, in hospitals, or in nursing homes, I occasionally drop by nearby Catholic churches. Removed from the incessant activity of the preceding visits, I thoroughly enjoy the quiet provided by these places of worship. I confidently assure myself that this house of God is truly sacred space. As I gaze at the tabernacle, I relish the moments of silent prayer with Jesus in the Blessed Sacrament. Here no one disturbs me. Here no one dares to interrupt my communing with the Lord. I glance at the altar and recall the previous Sunday's celebration of the Eucharist as both sacrament and sacrifice. As sacrament, the Eucharist provides nourishment for my journey through life. As sacrifice, the Eucharist recalls Jesus' self-giving in death for all. The altar is indeed a special kind of sacred space.

Gradually, however, I begin to realize that I have limited the notion of divine presence to sacred space. I feel that I must expand my view of that presence to include people. At this juncture my mind wanders back to the home, the hospital, the nursing home. Suddenly a light goes on! It now dawns on me that in leaving the home, the hospital, the nursing home for the church, I have really left God for God.

### Paul and the indwelling of the Holy Spirit

> Do you not know that you are the temple of God, and that the Spirit of God dwells in you? If anyone destroys God's temple, God will destroy that person; for the temple of God, which you are, is holy. (1 Cor 3:16-17)

Paul considers the church, that is, the Christian community, a spiritual temple because he finds there the most distinctive aspect of the Jerusalem temple. The temple is God's dwelling place on earth. It is nothing less than God's house. Moving from this notion of the Jerusalem temple, Paul concludes that the Christian community is the dwelling place of the Holy Spirit. Wherever there is a group of believers, a spiritual temple exists. In Paul's view his Corinthian Christians experience and radiate the divine presence.

Elsewhere in this same letter Paul expands this notion of the divine presence. He states that his converts in Corinth have been sanctified in Christ Jesus and are called, therefore, to be holy (1 Cor 1:2). He contrasts their former way of life (1 Cor 6:9-10) with their present status: "but now you have had yourselves washed, you were sanctified, you were justified in the name of the Lord Jesus Christ and in the Spirit of our God" (6:11).

Because God dwells in them, their bodies are holy, indeed temples of the Holy Spirit: "Do you not know that your body is a temple of the holy Spirit within you, whom you have from God, and that you are not your own?" (6:19).

### Returning to the home, the hospital, the nursing home

In the opening chapter I described the entrance into these three venues, especially for the first time, as experiencing a twilight zone. However, after reflecting on Paul's notion of the cultic nature of the Christian community and individual Christians, I feel I have gained a new perspective. Now I realize that all the venues of the physically and mentally impaired are temples of the Holy Spirit. They are communities of believers who reflect in diverse ways the radiance of God's presence. I realize that, like Jacob, I must announce: "How awesome this place is! This is nothing else but the house of God, the gateway to heaven!" (Gen 28:17). Like Moses, I must heed God's command: "Remove your sandals from your feet, for the place where you stand is holy ground" (Exod 3:5). Like Solomon, I must pray: "May your eyes be open night and day toward this house, the place of which you said, My name shall be there" (1 Kgs 8:29a).

It is as if I have put on new spectacles for the very first time. I no longer see deteriorating minds and bodies. I no longer observe the painfully slow gait of the age-ravaged residents. I no longer encounter inarticulate sufferers unable to meet by themselves their most basic needs. I now become acutely aware that while in the home, hospital, the nursing home, I am in church with my God because these physically and mentally impaired people radiate the divine presence. Indeed the Holy Spirit pervades this entire community of believers. In a truly real way I too share the experience of Jacob, Moses, Solomon, and Paul.

# God's Teammates

## Introduction

In the Bible God generally prefers a team approach in meeting the needs and addressing the problems of his people. For example, in establishing that people, God summons Abraham from Ur of the Chaldeans (southern Mesopotamia) and from there to Haran (northern Mesopotamia) and finally to the land of Canaan: "Go forth from your land, your relatives, and from your father's house to a land that I will show you" (Gen 12:1). God could have liberated the Israelites from their Egyptian brickyards by himself but he chose to depend on Moses: "Now indeed the outcry of the Israelites has reached me, and I have seen how the Egyptians are oppressing them. Now, go! I am sending you to Pharaoh to bring my people, the Israelites, out of Egypt" (Exod 3:9-10). When it is time to teach the people in the most complete way who God is, the Father sends the Son. When it is a question of preaching the Good News to the Gentiles, God calls Paul. The team approach generally wins out.

In addition to human beings, God chooses to depend on angels as his messengers or assistants. When Hagar runs away from her mistress Sarai, the Lord's angel appears to her in the wilderness, tells her to return to Sarai, and promises her a son (Gen 16:7-12). After the temptation in the desert, angels come and minister to Jesus (Matt 4:11; Mark 1:13). When Peter is in prison because of Herod Agrippa's persecution, the angel of the Lord arranges his escape (Acts 12:6-10).

Prophets occupy a conspicuous place on God's team. Rather than foretellers of the future, prophets function as God's spokespersons, communicating his message of reproach and/or hope. For example, in the eighth century BC, the prophet Amos must inform the people of the northern kingdom of Israel of its impending doom:

> She is fallen, to rise no more,
>     virgin Israel;
> She lies abandoned on her land,
>     with no one to raise her up. (Amos 5:2)

When God's people despair during their sixth-century exile in Babylon, God dispatches the prophet Second Isaiah with this message:

> Comfort, give comfort to my people,
>     says your God.
> Speak to the heart of Jerusalem and proclaim to her
>     that her service has ended. (Isa 40:1-2a)

### General role of the team players

Team playing for the ill involves a variety of participants—home caregivers, doctors, nurses, administrators, attendants, aides. They must aways bear in mind that their contributions in serving the physically and mentally impaired constitute a vocation, not simply a job that calls for punching in and punching out. (This applies especially to the home caregivers who are on call 24/7.) God summons them to assist him in providing for some of the most vulnerable people in the world. These people are very fragile and hence require special care and attention. A purely secular view would maintain that these men and women are not numbered among the most beautiful and hence are less deserving of their time and energy. A biblically oriented view, however, says otherwise.

### Faith as a first requirement

Faith entails an understanding and acceptance of the physically and mentally impaired from God's perspective. According to Genesis 1:26, all humans are created in God's image, after God's likeness. In Israelite religion, followers are forbidden to construct images of their God. However, humans get around this by imaging God in their entire being. In addition, God establishes men and women as players on his team. The author of Psalm 8 contrasts the heavens, moon, and stars with fragile human beings. But he quickly adds:

> Yet you have made him [humanity] little less than a god,
>   crowned him with glory and honor. (Ps 8:6)

As God's teammates, they must always see the physically and mentally impaired against the background of his creative intent.

> "When the Son of Man comes in his glory, and all the angels with him, he will sit upon his glorious throne, and all the nations will be assembled before him. And he will separate them one from another, as a shepherd separates the sheep from the goats. He will place the sheep on his right and the goats on his left. Then the king will say to those on his right, 'Come, you who are blessed by my Father. Inherit the kingdom prepared for you from the foundation of the world. For I was hungry and you gave me food, I was thirsty and you gave me drink, a stranger and you welcomed me, naked

and you clothed me, ill and you cared for me, in prison and you visited me.' Then the righteous will answer him and say, 'Lord, when did we see you hungry and feed you, or thirsty and give you drink? When did we see you a stranger and welcome you, or naked and clothe you? When did we see you ill or in prison, and visit you?' And the king will say to them in reply, 'Amen, I say to you, whatever you did for one of these least brothers of mine, you did for me.' Then he will say to those on his left, 'Depart from me, you accursed, into the eternal fire prepared for the devil and his angels. For I was hungry and you gave me no food, I was thirsty and you gave me no drink, a stranger and you gave me no welcome, naked and you gave me no clothing, ill and in prison, and you did not care for me.' Then they will answer and say, 'Lord, when did we see you hungry or thirsty or a stranger or naked or ill or in prison, and not minister to your needs?' He will answer them, 'Amen, I say to you, what you did not do for one of these least ones, you did not do for me.' And these will go off to eternal punishment, but the righteous to eternal life." (Matt 25:31-46)

In this scene of final judgment, Matthew reveals the implications of the vigilance and fidelity he has just expounded in his parables (Matt 24:32–25:30). Vigilance and fidelity are now reduced to recognizing the Son of Man in those the world labels of no account: the hungry, thirsty, naked, ill, and imprisoned. The standard or basis of judgment is the recognition or nonrecognition of these sisters and brothers of the Son of Man. In the dialogue with the two groups, what emerges is the criterion of identifying with Jesus. The Son of Man—the king/shepherd—identifies with all those who suffer. The least sisters and brothers are now those who experience any form of need. Fundamentally this is a theology of disguise. Salvation ultimately depends on recognizing or not recognizing Jesus in any person who suffers.

This theology of disguise applies in a very unique way to those serving the physically and mentally impaired. They are challenged to exercise the role of faith discussed above to all those in their care. They are urged to gaze deeper into the personhood of the physically and mentally impaired and discover there the image of Jesus. As experience shows, Jesus does not always reflect nice, neat, tidy images. Rather, the images can so often be upsetting and even revolting. In such instances their faith must enable them to adjust to the focus of this scene from Matthew. Jesus is a master of disguises.

### Compassion as a second requirement

The team members must complement their faith with compassion. Having discovered the presence of their brother Jesus, they must reach out to them in a caring, concerned way. In the Bible, the entrails or guts function as the seat of compassion. In the gospels there are more than a few instances of this deep emotion. Jesus demonstrates this profound capacity to reach out when he comes upon the widow of Nain who is about to bury her only son. His compassion prompts him to tell the widow not to weep. He steps forward, touches the coffin, and says: "Young man, I tell you, arise!" (Luke 7:14). The mourners quickly acknowledge that a great prophet is now in their midst.

> As they left Jericho, a great crowd followed him. Two blind men were sitting by the roadside, and when they heard that Jesus was passing by, they cried out, "[Lord,] Son of David, have pity on us!" The crowd warned them to be silent, but they called out all the more, "Lord, Son of David, have pity on us!" Jesus stopped and called them and said, "What do you want me to do for you?" They answered him, "Lord, let our eyes be opened." Moved with pity, Jesus touched their

eyes. Immediately they received their sight, and followed him. (Matt 20:29-34)

The title "Son of David" applies to Jesus as one who helps and cures the humble and despised. Matthew employs that title and the phrase "moved with pity" to underline his deep compassion. He views the two men as worthy recipients of his miraculous powers. They must not be silenced to please the crowd. Compassion is made of sturdier stuff. Perhaps the passage suggests that the team members should always be prepared to listen. Compassion does not consist in pleasing the crowd but alleviating the suffering of the physically and mentally impaired.

Jesus replied, "A man fell victim to robbers as he went down from Jerusalem to Jericho. They stripped and beat him and went off leaving him half-dead. A priest happened to be going down that road, but when he saw him, he passed by on the opposite side. Likewise a Levite came to the place, and when he saw him, he passed by on the opposite side. But a Samaritan traveler who came upon him was moved with compassion at the sight. He approached the victim, poured oil and wine over his wounds and bandaged them. Then he lifted him up on his own animal, took him to an inn and cared for him. The next day he took out two silver coins and gave them to the innkeeper with the instruction, 'Take care of him. If you spend more than what I have given you, I shall repay you on my way back.'" (Luke 10:30-35)

The Good Samaritan obviously discovers a value in the poor victim that the priest and Levite miss. The man's half-dead condition impacts the Samaritan to the point where he himself becomes the embodiment of compassion itself. Luke captures this sense of reaching out by devoting no less than three full verses to the details of the Samaritan's ministry. What must strike the team members in this parable is his total lack of concern for the victim's status, credentials, and the like. The Samaritan regards the tragic victim as a fellow human in need of dire help. Team members are challenged to emulate him by dismissing any and all questions of status or financial assets. Compassion must lead them to focus on the victim's needs, not on any notoriety that may accrue.

> So he got up and went back to his father. While he was still a long way off, his father caught sight of him, and was filled with compassion. He ran to his son, embraced him and kissed him. His son said to him, "Father, I have sinned against heaven and against you; I no longer deserve to be called your son." But his father ordered his servants, "Quickly bring the finest robe and put it on him; put a ring on his finger and sandals on his feet. Take the fattened calf and slaughter it. Then let us celebrate with a feast, because this son of mine was dead, and has come to life again; he was lost, and has been found." Then the celebration began. (Luke 15:20-24)

The father of the Prodigal Son dismisses all sense of hurt and betrayal. He focuses on only one thing, namely, the return of his younger son. He demonstrates deep compassion by running, embracing, and kissing him. However, his compassion does not stop here. He reinstates his son as part of the family by means of the robe, the ring, and the sandals. The party also symbolizes what it means to think in terms of others and not oneself. When dealing with difficult people who are physically and mentally impaired, the team members do well to adopt the strategy of the Prodigal Father. Forgetting all the hurts and heartaches of the past, he concentrates on only one object, namely, the return of his younger son. Team members must dare to emulate the father. They must focus on the needs of the moment, putting aside past difficulties and problems. Admittedly this is no easy task. Only genuine compassion makes it possible.

These three biblical passages address the team members as they serve the physically and mentally impaired. Compassion is more than mere pity. It is a quality in which one perceives the intrinsic worth of a human person and tries to honor that worth by direct intervention. The truly compassionate reach deep within themselves and share their gifts with others.

### Prophetic ministry

The faith-filled, compassionate people who serve the physically and mentally impaired also function as prophets. All too often we think of prophets as those solely concerned with predicting the future. In the Bible, however, prophets are God's proclaimers; they speak on behalf of God. This prophetic vocation is not limited to people, such as Isaiah, Jeremiah, Ezekiel, or Jesus. All the baptized receive this special calling. The caregivers of the physically and mentally impaired announce the Good News of Jesus in their homes as well as in the halls, corridors, and bedrooms of hospitals and nursing homes. To accomplish this, they do not require a bully pulpit. Whenever they help the physically and mentally impaired eat or walk, whenever they practice patience with difficult persons, whenever they offer a smile to the despondent, whenever they help with medications or perform other tasks, they fulfill their prophetic ministry. By these and other countless prophetic gestures, they implicitly evoke the response of the mourners at Nain that there is a prophet in their midst (Luke 7:16). Actions surpass words in prophetic ministry. St. Francis of Assisi instructed his followers to preach the Good News to everyone. He added: "If necessary, use words."

## The roles of clergy and pastoral ministers

Clergy, pastoral ministers, and the like play a significant role in assisting the physically and mentally impaired. By bringing the message of Jesus to homes, hospitals, and nursing homes, they proclaim the intrinsic goodness of human life no matter how disfigured and scarred it may appear on the surface. They announce that these people possess an inherent dignity because they are God's handiwork. They do not see them as so many objects of passing pity but as a chorus of believers who in their own unique way chant the praises of their God. By ministering to them, they reject the false premise that their suffering and that of their family and friends have no value.

Given the condition of the physically and mentally impaired, clergy, pastoral ministers, and the like must cultivate the virtues of patience and tolerance. They must always realize that this particular congregation cannot always respond like their healthy counterparts. They must dare to emulate the dedication and attentiveness of the home caregivers and professional staff. They must not only observe their generous service but also put it into practice in the other areas of their spiritual ministry. In this way home caregivers and professional staff serve as a mentoring body. They challenge clergy and pastoral ministers to learn from their performance and carry it over to all the other dimensions of their profession. The physically and mentally impaired, the team members, and the spiritual leaders thus constitute a trinity in which all interact and cross-fertilize their talents and gifts. All three groups are not only teachers but learners.

## Roles of family and friends

Family and friends naturally search for the reason for their family member's/friend's physical and mental impairment. They want to know specifically why God has punished their family member/friend and themselves with such pain, humiliation, and suffering. Given this state of mind, the book of Job may be instructive.

Job's friends prove to be anything but friends. Eliphaz, Bildad, and Zophar, the voices of orthodoxy, maintain that the cause of Job's misfortune is some sin or offense that he has committed. They recall the traditional doctrine of disciplinary suffering:

> Happy the one whom God reproves!
> The Almighty's discipline do not reject. (Job 5:17)

All Job has to do is simply acknowledge his fault and everything will be as before.

After citing their pious platitudes (see Job 12:4), Job accuses them of speaking falsely for God:

> But you gloss over falsehoods,
> you are worthless physicians, every one of you! . . .
> Is it for God that you speak falsehood?
> Is it for him that you utter deceit?" (Job 13:4, 7)

For Job the theology of the friends is mere fabrication: Job longs to be left alone. After all, he has done nothing wrong but inexplicably he is suffering enormously.

Ironically at the end of the book (chaps. 38–41) God responds by completely ignoring all of Job's questions. For the author these questions are simply wrong. The right question must deal with the element of paradox. Hence, God is able to afflict one who is righteous because he or she is righteous. The author seems to be suggesting that Job must learn to cultivate a sense of mystery. He must allow for a God of love and compassion who, bypassing the retribution equation of the friends, deals with humans in a concerned but paradoxical manner. This God is not the cold, impersonal Celestial Administrator. This God is a God of fidelity who refuses to be manipulated by all too neat human equations. God loves Job, but it is a love that does not provide answers to wrong questions.

This brief reflection on the book of Job will probably not satisfy many family members and friends of the physically and mentally impaired. They will always want an explanation that will clarify everything. However, such an explanation is beyond their reach; it is beyond all human understanding based on cause and effect. It may be helpful in such moments to ponder the mystery of the cross and the injustice of killing a totally innocent man. It makes no sense at all! After meditating on the cross, they must look to the empty tomb and its message of hope.

# Hope Springs Eternal

## Introduction

In his *Divine Comedy,* Dante Alighieri envisions the famous sign on the gates of hell as follows: "Abandon all hope, you who enter here." Family and friends of the physically and mentally impaired are easily tempted to transfer these words to homes, hospitals, and nursing facilities. Most readily acknowledge that there is little or no hope for recovery from serious physical and mental illness. They feel they must stoically accept this reality and soldier on as best they can. In this scenario hope is in seriously short supply.

Hope, however, has other dimensions. While there may be little or no hope of physical or mental recovery, there is the genuine hope of ongoing heavenly life. Such life is not "pie in the sky." As the notion of heaven develops in the New Testament, it emerges as a place where Jesus' extended family shares the company of Abraham, Isaac, and Jacob as well as Sarah, Rebekah, and Rachel. Heaven in this sense does not conjure up images of people parading about in white gowns supported by angel-like wings. The musical instrument of choice is not the harp. The entrance to this place is not the Pearly Gates where one must pass muster with St. Peter. Heaven means family reunion, sharing community with our loved ones and all the other members of Jesus'

extended family who are our family. Heaven is people-ori-
ented. Indeed it is often depicted as a banquet where God
or Jesus is the host (see Matt 8:11; Luke 22:29-30). Heaven
reflects our God's capacity to surprise us with unimaginable
Good News. As Paul puts it,

> "What eye has not seen, and ear has not heard,
>     and what has not entered the human heart,
>     what God has prepared for those who love him,"
> this God has revealed to us through the Spirit. (1 Cor 2:9-10)

The gospel of John uses "I am" images of Jesus such as I
am the Bread of Life or the Light of the World. These in turn
address the issue of hope, often hope of eternal life. With
these images, family members and friends of the physically
and mentally impaired can nourish their hope of heavenly
life for both their loved ones and themselves.

### The Bread of Life

So Jesus said to them, "Amen, amen, I say to you, it was not
Moses who gave the bread from heaven; my Father gives
you the true bread from heaven. For the bread of God is that
which comes down from heaven and gives life to the world."

So they said to him, "Sir, give us this bread always." Jesus
said to them, "I am the bread of life; whoever comes to me
will never hunger, and whoever believes in me will never
thirst. . . .

"Amen, amen, I say to you, whoever believes has eternal
life. I am the bread of life. Your ancestors ate the manna in
the desert, but they died; this is the bread that comes down
from heaven so that one may eat it and not die. I am the
living bread that came down from heaven; whoever eats this
bread will live forever; and the bread that I will give is my
flesh for the life of the world."

The Jews quarreled among themselves, saying, "How
can this man give us [his] flesh to eat?" Jesus said to them,

"Amen, amen, I say to you, unless you eat the flesh of the Son of Man and drink his blood, you do not have life within you. Whoever eats my flesh and drinks my blood has eternal life, and I will raise him on the last day. For my flesh is true food, and my blood is true drink. Whoever eats my flesh and drinks my blood remains in me and I in him. Just as the living Father sent me and I have life because of the Father, so also the one who feeds on me will have life because of me. This is the bread that came down from heaven. Unlike your ancestors who ate and still died, whoever eats this bread will live forever." (John 6:32-35, 47-58)

In 6:35-58 Jesus' Bread of Life discourse contains two components: the heavenly bread as his revelation or teaching (vv. 35-50) and this bread as the Eucharist (vv. 51-58). While John, unlike the Synoptics (Matthew, Mark, and Luke), does not have an institution of the Eucharist at the Last Supper, he develops the significance of the Eucharist in verses 51-58, drawing inspiration from the multiplication of loaves and fish (John 6:1-15). This second component parallels the first, enriching the theme of heavenly bread through the perspective of the Eucharist.

In response to the people's request for a sign to prompt their faith in him, Jesus notes that it is not Moses who gave their ancestors bread from heaven (manna). Rather, Jesus' Father gives them the true bread from heaven, specifically Jesus' revelation. Jesus assures them: "I am the bread of life; whoever comes to me will never hunger, and whoever believes in me will never thirst" (John 6:35). Those who accept Jesus in faith will hunger and thirst only for his revealing love. Jesus thereby identifies himself as the one who provides what is contained in the religious symbol of bread: "whoever believes has eternal life. I am the bread of life" (John 6:47-48).

In the Eucharistic component, Jesus states: "I am the living bread that came down from heaven." Jesus has not only become flesh, that is, human (John 6:51). He also gives his flesh and blood as food and drink for believers. Flesh implies the whole person as mortal and natural. Blood means the entire person as living. Jesus' flesh and blood are linked to the final resurrection: "Whoever eats my flesh and drinks my blood has eternal life, and I will raise him on the last day." Compared to Jesus as the living bread, the manna in the desert provides only a very weak analogy.

Both components in this Bread of Life discourse explode with overpowering messages of hope for the physically and mentally impaired as well as their loved ones and friends. They have the assurance of Jesus' revelation that, in believing in the Bread of Life, they will never hunger or thirst again. Jesus represents everything that is contained in the religious symbol of bread. Hence, Jesus will continue to nourish them provided they continue to cling to him in faith. Jesus supplies such nourishment especially in those moments when relationships with the physically and mentally impaired become strained and despair seems to be winning the day. However, the Bread of Life will assuredly grant those believers eternal life.

Eucharist must play a significant role both for the physically and mentally impaired as well as their loved ones and friends. Jesus' flesh and blood put all of them in intimate contact with him. Eucharist provides the necessary food and drink in their journey through life. But it has another facet: Jesus' flesh and blood are linked to the final resurrection. Jesus categorically states that on the last day he will raise all who share the Eucharist. In a sense, the believer has a foothold in two worlds: the earthly world with the pain and frustration of physical and mental impairment and the heavenly world with its ongoing association with the Bread of Life. In Eucharist, heaven and earth intersect.

**The Light of the World**

"While I am in the world, I am the light of the world." When he had said this, he spat on the ground and made clay with the saliva, and smeared the clay on his eyes, and said to him, "Go wash in the Pool of Siloam" (which means Sent). So he went and washed, and came back able to see. . . .

So they said to him, "[So] how were your eyes opened?" He replied, "The man called Jesus made clay and anointed my eyes and told me, 'Go to Siloam and wash.' So I went there and washed and was able to see." . . .

So they said to the blind man again, "What do you have to say about him, since he opened your eyes?" He said, "He is a prophet." . . .

It is unheard of that anyone ever opened the eyes of a person born blind. If this man were not from God, he would not be able to do anything." . . .

When Jesus heard that they had thrown him out, he found him and said, "Do you believe in the Son of Man?" He answered and said, "Who is he, sir, that I may believe in him?" Jesus said to him, "You have seen him and the one speaking with you is he." He said, "I do believe, Lord," and he worshiped him. Then Jesus said, "I came into this world for judgment, so that those who do not see might see, and those who do see might become blind." (John 9:5-7, 10-11, 17, 32-33, 35-39)

Jesus first uses this metaphor of light on the last day of the Feast of Tabernacles. On that occasion Jesus dramatically announces: "I am the light of the world. Whoever follows me will not walk in darkness, but will have the light of life" (John 8:12). Perhaps set against the background of the pillar of fire during the Exodus, this imagery of light illustrates his message or revelation. This light entails decision-making on the part of Jesus' audience. On the one hand, they can reject this light and choose to walk in darkness. On the other hand, they can opt to walk in the light of life by accepting Jesus and his message. The metaphor of Jesus as the Light of the World assumes added significance when one recalls that on the Feast of Tabernacles the temple becomes the light of the city of Jerusalem. As the Light of the World, Jesus dispels the darkness hovering over the physically and mentally impaired as well as their loved ones and friends.

Jesus uses his symbolism a second time in the account of the healing of the man born blind. Here Jesus informs his disciples: "While I am in the world, I am the light of the world." The cure of the man born blind will constitute the victory of light over darkness, thus vindicating Jesus' claim to be the light of the world. The contrast between the man born blind and the Pharisees/Jews is anything but subtle. While the man progresses gradually from darkness (blindness) to light (complete healing), the Pharisees/Jews move from initial halting acceptance to outright rejection of Jesus. Like the man born blind, the physically and mentally impaired as well as their loved ones and friends advance slowly but surely in their journey of hope.

Darkness and doubt often plague the lives of the physically and mentally impaired as well as their loved ones and friends. There seems to be no way out; everything is blacked out. Frustration increases as they try to cope with the thickening darkness. However, the account of the man born blind may offer a glimmer of hope. In that episode hope develops only gradually, step-by-step. Here hope consists in discovering the full identity of Jesus. The man born blind first speaks of Jesus as a man (v. 11), labels him a prophet (v. 17), acknowledges his origin from God (v. 33), and finally identifies him as the Son of Man (v. 38).

This painstaking course of action can overlap with the process of discovery for the physically and mentally impaired as well as family and friends. Darkness sets in when they first learn of the situation. Then perhaps a glimmer of hope breaks through the darkness when they realize the involvement of the Light of the World in their predicament. Although these experiences of light may flicker and fade, hope continues its relentless efforts to penetrate the remaining darkness. Hope, in the final analysis, is rooted in the Light of the World.

## The Good Shepherd

"I am the good shepherd. A good shepherd lays down his life for the sheep. A hired man, who is not a shepherd and whose sheep are not his own, sees a wolf coming and leaves the sheep and runs away, and the wolf catches and scatters them. This is because he works for pay and has no concern for the sheep. I am the good shepherd, and I know mine and mine know me, just as the Father knows me and I know the Father; and I will lay down my life for the sheep. I have other sheep that do not belong to this fold. These also I must lead, and they will hear my voice, and there will be one flock, one shepherd. This is why the Father loves me, because I lay down my life in order to take it up again. No one takes it from me, but I lay it down on my own. I have power to lay it down, and power to take it up again. This command I have received from my Father." (John 10:11-18)

In the Ancient Near East gods and kings were called shepherds because the ideal leaders committed themselves to the welfare and protection of their people (the sheep). This metaphor implies both authority over and responsibility to those in one's charge. In this passage, John looks back to Jesus' dispute with the Pharisees over the man born blind. In this scene Jesus contrasts himself with the Pharisaic leaders. The passage consists of three parts: the first parable of the ideal shepherd (vv. 11-13), the second parable of the ideal shepherd (vv. 14-16), and Jesus' laying down his life for his flock (vv. 17-18).

In the first parable Jesus unequivocally states his relationship to the sheep: "I am the good shepherd. A good shepherd lays down his life for the sheep." In this context, the hired hands are most likely the Pharisees. In the second parable Jesus again identifies himself as the good shepherd but adds: "I know mine and mine know me, just as the Father knows me and I know the Father" (John 10:14-15a). Knowing implies, not a purely cerebral knowledge, but a deeply personal knowledge between shepherd and sheep. The goal of this knowledge is to foster unity among all of Jesus' followers. The concluding verses perhaps connect this mission with Jesus' death and resurrection. The final verse shows that his death and resurrection reflect obedience to the Father's will. Jesus thus commits himself in full freedom to taking up his life again.

This brief passage projects a profound message of hope. Here John's audience learns that, as shepherd, Jesus will not hesitate to put his life on the line for the sheep. They further understand that Jesus is not constrained to die but submits himself freely to this ordeal out of obedience to the Father and in preparation for his resurrection. Furthermore, Jesus' followers confirm their hope in One who knows them personally and intimately.

Similarly the physically and mentally impaired as well as their loved ones and friends are not abstract ciphers in a heavenly ledger. Using the metaphor of shepherd and flock, the author of John assures them that they are the special objects of Jesus' loving care. Having endured the ordeal of crucifixion, Jesus can appreciate the frustration and anger experienced by the physically and mentally impaired and their loved ones.

It is this sense of intimate communion with Jesus that must energize the hope of the physically and mentally impaired and their families. They learn from John that Jesus will not permit them to be scattered and threatened. As the Good Shepherd, he has a vested interest in each of them. Just as Jesus enjoys the power to lay down his own life, he also has the power to take up the lives of all his sheep, especially the most fragile. This metaphor of shepherd must inspire the physically and mentally impaired and their families to pray:

> The LORD is my shepherd; . . .
> He guides me along right paths
> for the sake of his name. (Ps 23:1a, 3b)

### The Resurrection and the Life

When Jesus arrived, he found that Lazarus had already been in the tomb for four days. Now Bethany was near Jerusalem, only about two miles away. And many of the Jews had come to Martha and Mary to comfort them about their brother. When Martha heard that Jesus was coming, she went to meet him; but Mary sat at home. Martha said to Jesus, "Lord, if you had been here, my brother would not have died. [But] even now I know that whatever you ask of God, God will give you." Jesus said to her, "Your brother will rise." Martha said to him, "I know he will rise, in the resurrection on the last day." Jesus told her, "I am the resurrection and the life; whoever believes in me, even if he dies, will live, and everyone who lives and believes in me will never die. Do you believe this?" She said to him, "Yes, Lord. I have come to believe that you are the Messiah, the Son of God, the one who is coming into the world." (John 11:17-27)

In this passage John relates the scene of Jesus' meeting with Martha four days after the death of her brother. Martha is aware that, if Jesus had arrived earlier, Lazarus would not have died but that even at this moment the Father will not deny him anything. At this juncture Jesus reassures her that her brother will rise. Martha assumes that Jesus means the resurrection of the dead on the last day. Jesus responds to this limited hope in these words: "I am the resurrection and the life; whoever believes in me, even if he dies, will live" (John 11:25). Jesus then asks Martha whether she accepts this.

This scene in the Fourth Gospel considers the following question: if believing in Jesus means the attainment of eternal life (5:24), then how explain the death of faithful disciples? Jesus' self-identification as the resurrection and the life provides the answer to this question. Only by accepting Jesus on these terms can believers hope to enjoy eternal life and final resurrection. Paradoxically, Jesus as the resurrection and the life offers eternal life that transcends death but does not eliminate it.

Although the language in this scene emphasizes faith, hope is also clearly present. But it is a faith in Jesus as the resurrection and the life that generates hope in view of the death of the physically and mentally impaired and their survivors. Hope, like faith, is rooted in the One who defeats death in his resurrection. Transformed by this event, Jesus extends the message of hope to all his followers. Thus, the Resurrection impacts not only Jesus but all those who pin their hopes on him. The empty tomb reveals hope fulfilled for Jesus and hope to be fulfilled for the physically and mentally impaired as well as their family members and friends. The decidedly hopeful note in this passage is that Jesus himself is the resurrection and the life. The physically and mentally impaired as well as their families and friends must focus on this personal basis of hope, namely, one grounded in Jesus himself. This is a God who generates hope in his very person.

## Summary

These powerful images of Jesus as the Bread of Life, the Light of the World, the Good Shepherd, and the Resurrection and the Life speak to the needs and anxieties of the physically and mentally impaired as well as their family members and friends. These images are not simply beautifully crafted phrases intended to sugarcoat the reality of sickness and death. They are a lifeline of hope that endeavors to capture the reality of eternal life. These images also generate hope as family members and friends deal concretely with the erosion of physical and mental life. Under these images Jesus envisions his mission as one of providing genuine life: "I came so that they might have life and have it more abundantly" (John 10:10b).

# Index of Biblical Passages